BUDGIES
AS A NEW PET
BARRY MARTIN

1995 Edition

CONTENTS

Photos by Dr. Herbert R. Axelrod, Gary Duesler, Michael Gilroy, Harry V. Lacey, Louise Van der Meid, and Vogelpark Walsrode.

Published by
T.F.H. PUBLICATIONS, INC.
1 T.F.H. Plaza
Neptune, NJ 07753
Made in the USA

Introduction

In the last fifty years, the budgerigar has gradually replaced the canary as the most popular cage bird in the world. Millions of these charming little Australian parakeets have found their way into the homes of a countless number of families. Very few people, other than those living in the remotest regions, have never heard of or seen a budgerigar.

How is it that this tiny winged creature has stolen the hearts of so many people? Perhaps it is that the birds of the parrot family have a list of attributes rarely seen in other birds. Many people would like to own a parrot or a cockatoo but, for reasons of space, have to opt for something smaller. The budgerigar fits the role perfectly. It is a parrot with all of the desired attributes, but it comes in a reasonable size. It has colorful plumage and, with the myriad of captive mutations, is

Budgerigars are popular pets because they are pretty, entertaining, and easy to care for. In addition, they are ideal for a household that is unable to accommodate larger pets.

Two or more budgerigars kept together will bond to each other rather than to their owner, but they will keep each other happily occupied.

available in almost any color to suit any taste.

The budgerigar is easily tamed to sit on the finger and is friendly and entertaining. It does not have as raucous a voice as do many other parrots. It is also an excellent mimic of the human voice and other sounds. Moreover, it is extremely hardy. The budgie can be kept in an outdoor aviary year 'round even in cold winters, providing it has a dry, draft-proof shelter. It is also perfectly suited as a pet and companion. Few birds have as many positive qualities, which is why the budgerigar has myriad fans the world over.

Why do people keep birds in cages? This is a question often asked and difficult to answer concisely. Man, as a species, has always been regarded by scientists as an instinctive hunter and gatherer. At intervals in history, civilizations have attempted to make their hunting and gathering easier by domesticating food

different from its wild relative that it has become a new species. The domestic dog and the domestic cat are two such examples.

The most well-known domestic bird is the domestic fowl or chicken. It has been domesticated for 5,000 years or more. It is thought to be descended from the Red Jungle Fowl, *Gallus gallus*, still found in the jungles of Southeast Asia today. The domestic fowl was first developed for its meat and egg-producing qualities. The luxury of keeping fowl for ornamental or sporting (cock-fighting) reasons was probably out of the question to struggling humanity at the time. Today, thousands of captive generations have produced mutations bred specially for meat, egg laying or ornamental purposes. Many of the modern breeds or strains do not bear the slightest resemblance to the original wild fowl in size, shape or color.

Ample evidence in old documents, artifacts, and ornaments of early civilizations, in both the old and new worlds, indicates that various animals were

animals and growing vegetable crops. Though the hunting and collecting instincts have become ever more modified, and scientific methods have become more and more sophisticated, these instincts still remain in the subconscious.

Domesticating an animal means taking it from its wild habitat, keeping it in a controlled environment and breeding it for many generations. Over time, many of its wild characteristics are lost. In some cases, the domestic version of an animal is so kept for companionship, amusement or ornamental purposes. The ancient Egyptians left behind paintings and hieroglyphics referring to birds, including certain parrots not native to Egypt. The early Chinese and Japanese kept birds in fanciful bamboo cages so that they could wonder at their color and take pleasure in hearing their song. In South America, the Incas were known to keep and train certain parrots and macaws. Even today, some Amerindian tribes catch and tame wild parrots.

In India, aviculture was already in existence in the Middle Ages. Members of the nobility kept aviaries containing many species of birds, including parrots and parakeets. During the Middle Ages in Europe, native songbirds were kept as household pets. The canary, already bred in Spain in the 15th century, soon became a popular species. The first parrot-like birds to be brought to Europe expressly as cage birds were probably Indian Ring-necked Parakeets, obtained by Alexander the Great in his travels.

The budgerigar is a relative newcomer to aviculture. It was first brought to England by the naturalist and bird artist John Gould in 1840. The assumption is that the original birds were taken

Budgies are beautiful birds, exhibiting a variety of luminous colors. You may have your heart set on a bird of a particular color—which is perfectly fine—but your foremost consideration is to select a bird that is healthy, alert, and active.

from a wild nest because Gould's brother-in-law, Charles Coxon, hand-reared them. The budgerigars' readiness to breed in captivity soon led to their being produced as easily as canaries. Numerous offspring found their way into the homes of the rich. Later, as prices decreased, they became available to almost everyone. They soon spread to the European continent. There they were first bred in great numbers in Belgium and Holland, then France and Germany.

Large breeding

establishments came into existence throughout Europe, then in America and Japan. For a time, budgerigar breeding was big business. As the birds became more available to the general public, many small breeders replaced the larger entities. Today, countless breeders of budgerigars keep the market saturated. Most pet shops always have a few birds on hand.

This book is primarily for the beginner. It contains all the information necessary to acquire a pet budgie and care for it efficiently. It also caters to those persons who would like to establish an ornamental aviary and to those who want to try serious breeding.

Evolution, Classification, Biology

Bird fanciers of all kinds like to know background information about their chosen species. Such knowledge is not necessarily essential to successfully keep and breed budgerigars. Certainly, though, it gives insight into various ornithological matters and helps turn a novice into an expert. What follows, then, is a brief discussion of the evolution of birds, scientific classification and the biology of parrot-like birds, particularly the budgerigar.

Bird Evolution

Much of our knowledge about life-forms on earth has been gleaned from the study of fossils. These are like evolutionary fingerprints. They tell us about animals which existed at various periods in history and how they changed, by a system of evolution, into the animals we find on earth today. Until the middle of the 19th century, scientists and laymen alike generally thought that any variation in the form of a particular

Budgies are intelligent birds that will enjoy the play objects that you provide for them. Observing the behavior of your pet can be a fascinating and enjoyable part of your hobby.

species was purely incidental or accidental.

The English biologist Charles Darwin (1809-1882) created shock waves with his work, *The Origin of Species*, published on November 24, 1859. In it, Darwin suggested that all living organisms are related to one another by common ancestry; that all forms of life diverged from a single ancestral form over eons of time (now estimated at 3.8 billion years). At that time, the theory caused an uproar in scientific as well as ecclesiastical circles, as it implied that man evolved from the apes. Darwin's theory of evolution by natural selection is now widely accepted.

Natural selection, or 'survival of the fittest', is the hypothesis for the mechanism of evolution. It implies that all populations of living organisms transform over time to adapt to a changing environment. This is brought about as random, inheritable variations (mutations) occur by chance. Some of these variations allow individuals and their offspring to survive and reproduce more successfully than other creatures. The latter die out as they cannot compete with the more successful creatures.

Looking at bird evolution in particular, a clearer picture of the general mechanism emerges. The fossil record tells us that during the Triassic period (190 - 225 million years ago) the dry land was populated by insects, amphibians, reptiles and plants. There were no mammals and no birds as yet. Indeed, there were no flying vertebrates whatsoever. The only animals to conquer the air at the time were certain insects. The most numerous vertebrates on land were lizard-like reptiles. Most of these were carnivorous, feeding upon insects and other reptiles.

This was a time of tremendous competition for food; each species was continuously developing more efficient means of gaining sustenance. In order to catch their prey, the larger creatures had to increase their speed and the smaller one, paradoxically, had to increase their speed in order to escape. Some of the smaller reptiles took to the

trees to pursue their prey or to escape the larger terrestrial species. Those who failed in hunting, or escaping the hunter, invariably became extinct. The survivors passed on their superior genes to the next generation.

At the beginning of the Jurassic period (190 million years ago), the first flying reptiles appeared. They evolved from the more efficient leapers and gliders among the arboreal lizards. Flying surfaces between their limbs and elongated digits developed. The flying reptiles were collectively known as pterosaurs. They ranged in size from Rhampho-rhynchus, with a wingspan of about 60 cm (2 ft), to Pteranodon, with a wingspan of 7m (25 ft) or even more. The pterosaurs developed many species over their era of 135 million years. Toward the end of the Cretaceous period they became extinct.

It is suspected that the birds, appearing in the mid-Jurassic period (160 million years ago), were indirectly

referred to as being warm-blooded). This led to a more efficient metabolism and made birds more competitive than the reptiles for the available food.

The earliest fossil bird discovered so far is Archaeopteryx. Four fossils were unearthed in the Solnhofen limestone of Bavaria (Germany). One of these fossils is almost complete. It provided a great deal of information about bird evolution. The fossil shows both reptilian and avian characteristics, indicating that the earliest birds evolved from reptiles. Even today's birds still have scales on their legs and feet; close studies of feathers show a remarkable relationship to reptilian scales.

Unfortunately, much of our knowledge of the evolution of many bird families is incomplete. Good fossils are few and far between. This is because when a bird died, it was usually eaten by a scavenger and its bones were scattered far and wide. Fossilized single bones and bone fragments are continuously found by paleontologists. Fitting them all together to

responsible for this extinction. Surprisingly, the birds did not evolve directly from the pterosaurs; they probably developed from other kinds of lizards. Their method of conquering the air in flight was somewhat different from that of the pterosaurs. Instead of developing a membrane of skin to act as a flight surface, the reptilian scales developed into feathers. These not only allowed the animal to fly; they also insulated the body against extremes of temperature. This insulation allowed birds to develop homoiothermy: the ability to maintain the body temperature at a constant level, whatever the temperature of the environment (erroneously form a whole skeleton, though, is worse than doing the most difficult jigsaw puzzle that has most of the pieces missing.

What we do know is that assorted species of bird radiated into every niche on the planet capable of supporting life. Birds are found in the Arctic and the Antarctic, the deserts and the mountain tops, fresh water and salt water, forest, bushland and heathland. They range in size from the tiny hummingbirds, 5 cm (2 in) in length, to the mighty ostrich, standing at 2 m (6 ft) in height. They exploit all forms of food; some birds are primarily insect eaters, others subsist on seeds, fruit or green food. Still others are scavengers and fishers, hunters and grazers, nectar feeders and filter feeders. Each species has evolved its own unique way of obtaining food. The shape of the beak, type of feet, methods of flying, walking and swimming are all designed to facilitate a bird's success in its own field.

Classification

The budgerigar's scientific name is *Melopsittacus undulatus*. Such scientific classifications are a necessary identification term because each plant and animal has different common names in different languages. For example, in German the budgerigar is known as Wellensittich, in Dutch, Grasparkiet. In French, Polish and Japanese he is known as something else. Even in English, although budgerigar (derived from an Australian Aboriginal dialect) is the most widespread label, there exist an abundance of other common names. These include modifications of the Aboriginal name, such as Budgerygah and Betcherrygah. Also, a

Wild budgerigars live in large flocks; it is therefore important that the owner of the pet budgie have enough time to spend with a singly kept bird.

number of English names exist, including Green Grass Parakeet, Shell Parrot, Zebra Parrot, Canary Parrot, Scallop Parrot and Lovebird. (This last name is more commonly used to describe the small African Lovebird parrots of the genus *Agapornis*).

Consider the vast array of common names of animals and plants. There are over 8500 species of modern birds alone! Hence, it is not difficult to understand why early zoologists and botanists had such difficulty in communicating the results of their research from one country to the next. Then came a breakthrough in scientific classification. The Swedish botanist Karl von Linné (1707-1778) devised the binomial system of scientific nomenclature and published it in his *Systema Naturae*. The system dictated that each species (the most natural and basic group of similar individuals which freely interbreed) be given a generic and a specific name. As Latin and classical Greek were the main international languages used by scholars at the time, these were the languages used to create the majority of scientific names. Such names would be international and were intended to be recognized by scientists whatever their native tongue. For example, the Sulphur-crested cockatoo is known scientifically as *Cacatua galerita*. The first name is that of the genus, the second that of the species. There are other species in the genus Cacatua: *Cacatua leadbeateri, Cacatua roseicapilla,* etc. All of these species show certain similarities warranting their

Inexpensive to maintain, the budgie, also known to some as the parakeet, is among the easiest of all birds to tame and enjoy as a pet.

placement in the genus.

Genera are placed in larger categories in ascending sequence. These include families, orders, classes and so on. Each classification is based on similarities, or differences, in the various groups. To illustrate the system more clearly, the following table shows the classification of our chosen species, the budgerigar.

Kingdom: Animalia
        All Animals
Phylum: Chordata
        All Chordates
Subphylum: Vertebrata
        All Vertebrates
Class: Aves
        All Birds
Order: Psittaciformes
        All Parrots,
        Cockatoos, Etc.
Family: Psittacidae
        All Parrots
Genus: *Melopsittacus*
        Budgerigars
Species: *undulatus*

You can see that the budgerigar is a bird in the parrot family. However, unlike cockatoos, the budgie has a genus all to itself. There are no other species regarded by ornithologists as sufficiently closely related to the budgerigar to be

At first, your budgie may be reluctant to be held, but with time he will become accustomed to your touch.

included in the genus Melopsittacus. Moreover, there are currently no recognized geographical variations or subspecies.

Biology

A basic familiarity with bird biology and a more thorough understanding of the particular biology of the budgerigar will give you a more positive attitude about its captive care and breeding.

The upright, bipedal posture of birds was already established in their reptilian ancestors. Most of the typical bird characteristics are related to its ability to fly. Although there are several flightless birds today (ostrich, kiwi, penguin), it can be said that all birds, at some evolutionary stage, were capable of flight.

The specializations for flight include fusion and elongation of the wrists and fingers, providing support for the flight feathers. The skeleton is strong, but remarkably light. Many of the bones are hollow, containing extensive air cavities criss-crossed with netlike bracings for added strength. The most highly developed flight muscles are found in active fliers, like pigeons, making up half the body weight. The ancestral reptilian jaw has been dramatically reduced in weight to form a light, horny beak. These vary enormously according to the feeding habits of a particular bird species. A typical bird neck is long and flexible. The bones of the pelvis, rib cage and vertebra are fused into a semi-rigid unit. The breast bone is greatly enlarged, possessing a keel to which the large flight (breast) muscles are anchored. The tail is much reduced, having only four vertebrae. The feet are adapted, in various ways, for swimming, grasping, running, digging, gripping or perching.

The feathers provide flight surfaces and insulate the body against temperature extremes. The color of the plumage is important in species recognition and plays a part in courtship. The heart is four-chambered, efficient in pumping the blood around the body and maintains a high gas exchange in conjunction with the lungs and the air sacs. Birds are homoiothermic (warm-blooded), in that they are able to maintain their body temperature at a relatively constant level. It is usually higher, but not invariably so, than that of the environment.

Budgerigars belong to the order of parrots, Psittaciformes, and the family Psittacidae, in which there are some 328 species in 77 genera. The parrots have a pan-tropical distribution, but are particularly numerous in the Australasian region. Although they have instantly recognizable general features, the parrot-like birds vary greatly in size. The diminutive pygmy parrots, Micropsitta, at 10 cm (4 in) are smaller than sparrows, and the giant Hyacinthine Macaw, *Anodorhynchus hyacinthinus*, reaches lengths of 100 cm (39 in).

Most species of parrot are brightly colored. Many are excellent mimics of the human voice as well as other sounds. Most are relatively intelligent. All these factors make many of the species highly desirable as pets. Although they differ tremendously in color and size, parrots have many anatomical features in common with each other. A major characteristic is the robust beak. It reminds one of a bird of prey, but it is adapted for completely different purposes. The beak of the parrot is set higher, is shorter and more curved than that of a raptor. The upper mandible curves down

A well-balanced diet is an important factor in your budgerigar's health and well-being.

sharply over the lower one, and the former is provided with horizontal grooves. These grooves help the bird grip seeds more efficiently and they play a part in keeping the front of the lower mandible sharp. The parrot's tongue is usually large and fleshy. It is used to manipulate seed into a convenient position for de-husking. Some parrots (like lorikeets), however, have a 'brush tongue', specially adapted for removing pollen and nectar from flowers.

The feet of parrots are zygodactylous: the four toes are paired, two facing the front and two to the rear. (The vast majority of birds have three toes facing forward and one to the back.) This condition gives parrots a unique gripping power suited to clambering about in vegetation and searching for food. In some species, not including the budgerigar, the foot is also used to pick up items of food and hold them to the beak.

The Wild Budgerigar

The wild budgie is a small grass parakeet. It ranges in length from 17.5 to 18.5 cm (6.8 - 7.3 in). The sexes are similar in appearance. In adults, though, the cere (the bare, fleshy area above the beak and around the nostrils) of the cock is bright blue, while that of the female is brown or a faint bluish-brown. The back of the crown, the back and sides of the neck and the wings are barred black and yellow. The bars are narrow on the head and progressively widen onto the wings. The rest of the body is predominantly bright green. The front of the crown and the face are yellow. Some of the cheek feathers are tipped with violet. There is a series of black spots ringing the throat. The flight and tail feathers are blue-brown to blue-green. The beak and the feet are gray. The iris of the eye is white. Immature birds are more dull in appearance than the adults, and the black spots on the throat are ill-defined or absent. Adult plumage is acquired after the first molt, occurring around four months of age.

Budgerigars are Australian natives. They are found throughout the whole interior of the continent. However, the birds are scarce or absent from coastal

"Budgerigars are Australian natives. They are found throughout the whole interior of the continent."

areas of the extreme north, including Cape York, east of the Great Dividing Range, most of the southern coastal strip and Tasmania. They are nomadic creatures, their movements and breeding following the flushes of seeding grasses throughout September. Budgerigars remain in certain areas for long periods as long as the conditions are suitable.

They are gregarious, living in flocks of up to 100 birds. Sometimes, dictated by seasonal conditions, much larger flocks form. They are

The ability of the budgie to imitate the human voice and other sounds has endeared it to millions of people all around the world. (Employing a microphone during your pet's vocal training sessions is by no means a necessity.)

the arid zone. Many birds migrate to the south in the spring and remain for the summer. They breed from August to January and then depart for the north in the fall. In the northern areas, the birds may breed in the dry season from June to well coordinated in take-off, changes in direction and landing. They feed largely on seeding grasses, but also take other herbs. Budgies are not particularly specialized in choice of foods, even when rearing the young. They feed close to the ground in

groups, each bird independently foraging at its own plant.

At night, budgerigars usually roost in green trees, often close to water courses. They change their roosting site each night. They awake before dawn, with much preening and calling, then make their way to the feeding grounds at sunrise. They feed for most of the day, but peak times seem to be early morning and late afternoon. They are efficient at retaining water and usually drink only when it is very hot and dry. They swoop down to a watering hole in droves, immersing their heads in the water and rapidly slaking their thirst with gulping motions, before quickly flying off. Towards evening they rise in spectacular display flights skimming, turning and calling loudly, before settling down to roost for the night.

Breeding Cages

Most budgie pairs will readily breed in an all-wire cage if you provide a nest box. The majority of breeders, though, prefer to give them enclosed box cages with wire fronts for this purpose. The minimum dimensions of a breeding cage are 75 x 37.5 x 45 cm high (30 x 15 x 18 in). Such a cage can also be used as a stock cage for up to six non-breeding birds. Cages of various sizes are available from your local avicultural suppliers.

Many breeders like to construct their own breeding or stock cages. The wire cage fronts can be bought in several sizes. All you need do is to fabricate a plywood box to fit the front. A space should be left near the bottom of the front so that a sliding floor tray can be fitted. The top, bottom and ends of the cage are best made from 12 mm (0.5 in) thick plywood (exterior quality plywood is more

durable). The back can consist of 6 mm (0.25 in) ply. Take into account the thickness of the wood when measuring or you will end up with gaps or parts sticking out where they should not be. Many do-it-yourself stores provide facilities for cutting plywood accurately to size at no extra cost. The timber is assembled into a cage using wood glue and

sliding floor tray may be made from thin plywood, sheet aluminum or plastic. The latter may be obtainable in appropriate sizes from your pet supplier.

The nest box is best fitted to the outside of the cage. This affords the budgies more room in the cage. Access to and from the nest box is gained by cutting a hole about 4 cm (1.5 in) in diameter in the cage side.

Indoor Aviaries

An indoor aviary can be installed or constructed in any part of the house. Many types are on the market. These include an 'aviary on wheels' and prefabricated aviary panels. The panels can be arranged in many shapes and sizes. The most satisfactory type of indoor aviary is built-in, usually in an alcove or spare room. A battery of such aviaries is ideal if you contemplate breeding budgies year 'round. An advantage of indoor aviaries over outdoor ones is that they do not require a roof (they can go from floor to ceiling) or a shelter. The do-it-yourselfer can easily construct indoor aviaries from 5 x 5 cm (2 x 2

One of the most important considerations in planning an aviary is the provision of adequate flight space for the birds.

panel pins. When the glue has dried, you should have a very strong structure.

The cage front is securely fixed into place using brackets. It should be placed in such a way that it can be easily removed for cleaning or maintenance. The grille will already have an access door fitted into it; possibly, also gaps for food and water receptacles. Two perches provide for exercise. The

in) timber poles. These are screwed and plugged to the inner walls of the room and the appropriate pieces added. Wire netting attached to the inside of the framework covers the timber to prevent the birds from chewing it up.

Ideally the aviary door should not be higher than 150 cm (5 ft). As birds tend to fly upward when disturbed, they are less likely to escape over your head if the door is set low. For additional safety, install a safety porch at the aviary entrance; in the case of several aviaries, at the door to the room. A single aviary can be made into an extremely attractive feature in the home living area. Although it is futile to have plants inside the aviary, house plants can be placed around the aviary for a decorative effect.

The aviary floor can be just plain boards. Hardboard and plywood are favored so that the fewest seams exist. This minimizes cracks where disease organisms can harbor and multiply. It also makes cleaning operations that much easier. For a little extra expense, a plain vinyl or linoleum floor covering can be added. Be sure that there are no exposed edges

Perches are a very important part of a budgie's aviary (or cage) furnishings. Your pet shop dealer carries a variety of perches that are suitable for your pet.

that your birds could gnaw. Such a floor is easily swept and washed with a mild solution of bleach at regular intervals. When the floor is dry, sprinkle a thin layer of bird sand over it. This helps to eliminate the adhesion of droppings. Indoor aviaries can be of almost any size. The minimum dimensions for housing three pairs of budgies is 150 cm long x 100 cm broad (5 ft x 3 ft) and ceiling height.

Room Aviaries

A room aviary is similar to an indoor aviary, except that the birds have an entire room to themselves. A room aviary is superb for fanciers wishing to breed their birds on the colony system. To prevent escapes, wire-mesh screens are placed over the windows. In this way the windows can be opened for fresh air. It is also recommended to erect a safety porch at the room entrance. In a room aviary, birds have greater opportunity to exercise than they have in a small aviary. It is also easier to clean a whole room than confined spaces.

Outdoor Aviaries

The most suitable kind of accommodation for budgerigars is an outdoor aviary. Budgies are remarkably hardy birds once acclimated. By providing a dry and draft-proof shelter and a balanced diet, they may be kept without supplementary heating, even in unpleasant temperate winters. However, should temperatures fall below 5 C for some time, it is wise to install a small heater - just large enough to keep the shelter frost-free.

An outdoor aviary consists of two sections: a flight and a shelter. The flight is exposed to the weather; the shelter must have windows as birds may refuse to enter a completely dark space. Aviaries may be built in blocks of two or more. This is particularly important if selective breeding is contemplated. It is also possible to build flights attached to an existing shed or other building. These structures act as ready-made shelters which can be modified as necessary. The enclosed part of the shelter can have areas constructed as described for the indoor

aviary. Leave space for viewing the birds and to store food and equipment.

Siting:

Careful consideration must be given to the siting of the outdoor aviary. Be sure to get the approval of the local town planning board. Do not block a neighbor's view, cut out light or cause any other nuisance. Ideally, discuss your intentions with your neighbors at the outset and get their approval. It is better to get their co-operation now than to risk having to remove the aviary later.

The aviary should be positioned so that it is sheltered from cold winds; yet it should receive a fair quota of sunlight. A dense hedge or a solid wall at the rear of the structure, if possible, has a variety of

You may become so taken with the hobby that you will wind up with several budgies. Keep in mind that crowding the birds into too small quarters will make them nervous and unhappy.

functions. Such a back wall provides a feeling of security for the budgies while offering protection from the elements. A hedge also provides an attractive backdrop for the birds.

The Aviary Base:

A short brick or concrete block wall at the base of the aviary is optimal. It gives a solid foundation to the aviary and helps prevent timber from rotting by keeping it elevated. Additionally, it stops vermin from burrowing under the edge of the frame and just makes the entire system more attractive. The dimensions of the wall depend on the size of the aviary. If you purchase prefabricated aviary panels, the measurements must be exact. If you construct your own panels, these can be made to size after the wall is built.

The aviary dimensions are a matter of personal choice and available space. A suitable minimum floor area for the flight is about 3 x 1.5 m (10 x 5 ft). Choose fairly level ground and dig a foundation trench 25 cm deep x 25 cm wide (10 x 10 in). Drive wooden pegs into the floor of the trench,

ensuring that the top of each peg is level by using a level and a straight-edge. Prepare concrete (1 part cement, 2 parts sand and 4 parts gravel mixed with water to a workable consistency). Pour it into the trench until it reaches the tops of all the pegs. Tamp it down with a

All birds, not just budgies, are susceptible to drafts and fumes. Keep this in mind when you are selecting the site for the cage or aviary.

piece of flat timber until reasonably smooth. Now allow it to partially set. After four or five hours, scratch the surface of the concrete with the point of a trowel to provide a key for the brick work. At least 24 hours must pass before commencing with the wall.

The wall need not be higher than 22.5 cm (9 in). This is about equivalent to the height of three standard bricks or one concrete block. Using cement or mortar (1 part cement to 4 parts building sand, mixed with water to a workable consistency), erect the brick or block courses. Ensure they are level. Upright bolts should be set between the bricks at intervals around the top of the wall. They must be long enough to be firmly cemented into the wall and to pass through the base plates of the flight panels.

The Flight:

Allow at least 48 hours for the cement to set thoroughly before bolting the flight panels into position. Flight panels may be fabricated from timber 3.75 cm (1 in) square. The timber needs to be treated with a good quality wood preservative and to dry before securing joints. The height of the frames should not be less than 1.8 m (6 ft). This gives the aviary an overall height of 2.025 m (6 ft 9 in). The most suitable mesh to use for the panels is galvanized weld-mesh. This is more

"The aviary dimensions are a matter of personal choice and available space."

rigid than wire netting, easier to attach tidily and will not rust. Do not use a mesh size greater than 1.25 x 2.5 cm (1/2 x 1 in) or mice can gain entry. Attach the mesh to the inside of the timber using small, galvanized staples. The entire inside of the frames - to the edge - must be covered with the mesh. This prevents the birds from gnawing at the timber.

Once complete, place the frames in position on the base wall. Holes should be drilled in the base plates to fit the upright bolts. After bolting each individual frame to the base, the panels can be joined to each other using more bolts or screws. Finally, the roof panel is fitted. You will probably require some assistance to do this. Cover the roof and the back walls of the flight with plastic sheeting, for about one third of its length from the shelter. The birds can then remain outside in inclement weather without adverse effects.

The flight floor can be covered with turf which can be renewed when it becomes worn or soiled. As an alternative, the floor can be covered with a 5 cm(2 in) layer of coarse sand. This can be raked daily and replaced as needed. For large colonies of budgerigars, a drainable, solid concrete floor allows easy sweeping or hosing down.

The Shelter:

The two mandatory requirements of a shelter are that it is dry and that it is draft-proof. It can be constructed from almost any material, including timber, brick, cement block and aluminum panels. Tongued and grooved cedar boarding is an attractive constituent. It is often used in fashioning garden sheds, bird rooms and aviary shelters. It is easy to work and alter for individual demands. Such a construction should, like the flight, be set on a low foundation wall. It is always best to completely concrete the floor of the shelter. Be sure to include a drain so that the floor can be periodically hosed down. With a few modifications, an existing building can give rise to an aviary shelter.

If an access door is made directly from the shelter into the flight, there is no need for a door and a safety porch into the outside part of the flight. The minimum floor area for the shelter is 1.5 x 1.5 m (5 x 5 ft). It is best to include an access corridor at the back or side of the indoor part of the aviary. This acts as a safety porch. It also allows you to view birds, carry out chores and store food and equipment in a dry environment.

Windows are a must in the shelter because budgies will not enter a dark area (other than a nest box). Windows to the indoor flight should be protected on the inside with wire-mesh. This prevents the birds from flying into the glass, sustaining injury, and allows the windows to be open for fresh air without a bird escaping.

Good ventilation is vital. On a hot day, the inside of the shelter can quickly reach high temperatures. Therefore, two or three adjustable air vents should be located in the walls. In this way, mild ventilation is available even in the winter. Place the vents in a position where they will not expose the budgies to direct drafts.

The birds commute between the shelter and the flight by means of a 'pophole.' This should be an opening about 22.5 x 22.5 cm (9 x 9 in) situated near the top of the shelter. A sliding door, operated from the outside of the flight by a lever or chain, allows you to

Your budgie's housing should not be located in direct sunlight. Some sunlight in the cage or aviary is fine as long as the bird has a shaded area to go to as well.

Budgerigars love to gnaw, and a wood perch is quite likely to be the object of this activity. Check the condition of your pet's perch regularly, and replace it when it shows signs of wear.

lock the birds into the shelter at night or to catch a bird, if necessary. Should you have several aviaries together, it is useful to have controllable popholes leading from one enclosure into the next. The birds can be manipulated between aviaries in this manner. A small platform just below the pophole on either side helps the birds to enter and exit.

The inside of a timber shelter should be lined with hardboard or plywood to prevent drafts from coming through the cracks. Brick or building block shelters are preferably lined with a smooth coating. The inside walls can be painted with a light colored, non-toxic emulsion paint. This encourages cleanliness, reflects illumination and allows you a better view of the birds. The advantage of emulsion paint is that it can be washed and quickly have a new coat applied when needed.

The roof of the shelter should be well constructed. The eaves should overlap the walls to protect both the walls and the birds from rainy weather. The roof should slope away from the flight. It is also advisable to have a gutter and a drainpipe. For wooden shelters, a good grade of exterior plywood panels covered with a good grade of roofing felt are ideal. Brick or block structures may have decorative tiled roofs.

Perches:

Permanent hardwood perches can be affixed across the width of the shelter and the flight. Place one at each end of the flight at slightly different heights. The budgies will benefit greatly from the exercise provided by the maximum flying distance. Perches of varying thickness further exercise the feet and keep the claws worn down to a reasonable length.

Natural perches, cut from the boughs of non-poisonous trees, are decorative and beneficial to the budgies' diet. The birds will also delight in stripping off the bark. As the perches become chewed up and unsightly, simply replace them with fresh ones. Take care in your selection of such perch material, though. Remember that certain trees and shrubs (laburnum, yew, oleander) are poisonous. It is therefore safest to cut branches from fruit trees known to have not been treated with insecticides. Oak, beech, elder, and maple trees are also acceptable. Be sure that all perches are firmly attached to the aviary structure to avoid accidents.

Despite its hardiness, a budgie can be adversely affected by extreme temperature variations.

Budgies As Pets

The budgerigar is probably the world's most popular cage bird. It tames readily and has an endearing personality. The budgie is not as vociferous as some other parrots. However, in most cases, it can be taught to repeat words and phrases, mimic other sounds and whistle simple tunes.

Select a bird which has just left the nest and is able to feed itself. These chicks are more easily tamed and trained than mature birds. At this young age, though, it is difficult to distinguish the sexes. So if you prefer a particular sex, rely on the dealer to help you. Some dealers offer a guarantee that if the bird turns out to be other than what you expected, he will exchange it.

Cocks are usually preferred because they are more apt to talk than hens. Whether a bird turns out to be a good, mediocre or poor mimic, though, is really a matter of luck; each individual bird has degrees of ability and mood. But talker or not, nearly all budgerigars become tame and loving pets. Both sexes are an equally good choice.

Place your new pet immediately in its cage.

Open the cage door and place the lid of the traveling box against it. Quickly open the lid and allow the bird to hop out of the box and into the cage.

If possible, bring the bird home in the morning so he has all day to adjust. This move to a new home is one of the most traumatic moments in your bird's life.

for a couple of days. This is a typical reaction of a nervous bird.

Taming

Leave the bird in peace for the initial 24 hours. Distracting movements and loud noises should be kept to a minimum. After this settling-in period, the sooner the taming begins, the

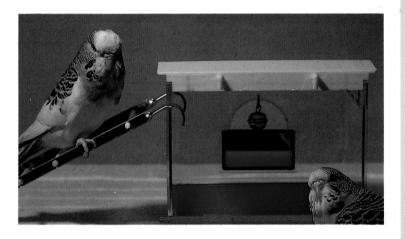

Bird toys such as those pictured here will provide your budgie with ample opportunity for fun and exercise—and you will be amused by your pet's antics!

Do not allow other pets to frighten it; keep away boisterous children. The first few days are a time of getting acquainted for both the bird and for the family.

Observe the bird closely for the first couple of hours. Be sure that he can find his food and water dishes. Do not be alarmed, though, should the bird refuse to eat

better. Talk to the bird quietly and reassuringly each time you approach the cage. Utter its name slowly and clearly as often as possible.

Very slowly put your hand through the cage door and move it towards the budgie. The moment it panics, freeze your movement until the bird is settled again. All the while, speak and whistle softly to your pet. Stretch your index finger towards its breast. If the bird panics, remove your hand and try again. Repetition and patience are the secrets to success.

A bird particularly reluctant to sit on your finger can be tamed with a short stick or dowel. Initially, the perch can be left in the cage so that the bird becomes completely accustomed to it.

Eventually the bird will permit you to stroke its breast. Next, place your index finger at the base of the breast and give a gentle nudge. As the budgie is thrown off balance, it should step forward and onto your finger. It may appear to you at first that the bird is going to bite. Do not panic, though. It is more likely that the budgie is simply using its beak for balance as it steps up. Once the bird is perched on your finger, get it used to motion by moving your hand about the cage. Let your new friend sit on your finger several times before removing it from the cage.

All caged budgerigars should be given free flying time every day. Before allowing a bird access to your living area, though, the room

To make sure that your budgerigar's attention is focused on you during a training or taming session, mirrors and other distractions must be removed from the training area.

must be bird-proofed! Be sure that all doors and windows are closed. Should even a tame budgie escape into the great outdoors, it is almost impossible to capture it again. Cover mirrors and windows so that the bird does not fly full force into them. Open fires, hotplates and boiling foods jeopardize the safety of your pet. Even if the fire is out, do not let your bird have access to a chimney flue. Other animals should be removed from the room; even the most trustworthy cats and dogs may lick their lips at the prospect of a budgie for dinner!

Remember also that budgies like to chew. Although not as destructive as some other parrot species, budgerigars can do a fair amount of damage to chewable items. Put papers, books and plants out of reach. Periodically check any exposed wiring for signs of wear. Secure or remove valuable objects that can be tipped and broken.

Training

As soon as your budgie is hand-tame, further training should continue. Speech

training can be done both when the bird is in the cage and while he is on your finger. Continually repeat the word or simple phrase you want the budgie to say. (The budgie's name and address are good things for it to know should it escape at some time.) Speak in a slow and clear manner and teach only one thing at a time. Do not introduce new pieces of vocabulary until the current one is mastered or the bird will be confused. Remember to reinforce previous words and phrases learned. Once a budgerigar has mastered one word, others are usually learned quite rapidly. Lots of praise and a tasty tidbit make encouraging rewards.

A budgie can be trained to

The first time that your budgie steps willingly onto your hand will be a very special experience. Successfully taming and training a bird requires much time and patience on your part, but the reward is worth it.

perform tricks as well as to learn to talk. You should have no trouble getting the bird to come to your hand on command. You can train it to jump from one finger to the other, or from your finger to your shoulder and onto your head! Your budgie should, of course, be trained to return to its cage as soon as playtime is over.

To get the bird to return to the cage, get it onto your finger or a small dowel. Slowly carry the budgie to the cage. After a time, it will understand your intent and jump into the cage of its own accord. The bird can even be trained to return to the cage from anywhere in the room at the utterance of a simple command.

Toys for Budgerigars

A bird which spends long periods of time in its cage needs 'toys' for entertainment. Pet shops offer an assortment of safe toys, though budgies will play with almost anything. Toys for purchase include mirrors, bells, and ladders. A bird may admire, talk to or even attack its own image in a mirror. (During training sessions, the mirror should be removed from the cage. Otherwise, the budgie might become so enamored of itself that it pays no attention to you!)

Objects found about the house can be great fun for your bird. Small twigs, ping-pong balls, bobbins and thread spools are terrific. A budgie will spend many happy hours chewing, pushing and tossing its toys about. Just be sure that any item offered to your pet is non-toxic, too large to swallow and cannot be broken into small pieces.

Budgerigar **N**utrition

Nutrition is the study of the processes of growth, maintenance and repair of the living body dependent upon the intake of food. A definition of food is any solid or liquid which, when swallowed, does a number of things. It provides materials from which the body produces heat, work or other forms of energy. It furnishes material allowing for growth, repair or reproduction. Also, it supplies substances which help in the mechanisms regulating the production of energy or the processes of growth, repair, and reproduction.

The study of diets can be extremely complex, but a basic knowledge of a budgerigar's specialized diet is important to your pet's health. Depending upon the species, the diet is constituted from a variety of foods. Each food contains one or more of certain groups of essential materials.

These materials are known as nutrients. A proper dietary balance is necessary for any animal to function correctly and maintain good health.

Essential Nutrients
Fortunately, the

In addition to your parakeet's basic diet, specialized mixes and treats are available from your local pet shop. You can feed a different one each day so that your pet has plenty of variety. Photo courtesy of Kaytee.

budgerigar is not a complex feeder. It is able to obtain all of its essential nutrients from a relatively minor array of foods. A balanced diet must contain the following nutrients in sufficient quantities.

Carbohydrates:

These provide the body with energy and may also be converted into body fat. They are composed of the elements carbon, hydrogen and oxygen in various molecular combinations. There are three major groups of carbohydrates:
1. Sugars, which are water-soluble and easily digestible. They are found naturally in fruits and plant juices.
2. Starches, which are not water-soluble. They are first converted into sugars by the digestive juices so that they may be assimilated. They are a major component of seeds, the budgie's staple diet.
3. Cellulose, which is indigestible to many

animals, but provides valuable fibrous bulk during the digestive process. It is common in all plant material.

Fats:

Like carbohydrates, fats consist of carbon, hydrogen and oxygen, but in differing proportions. They provide energy and help insulate the body against extremes of temperature. Additionally, they act as shock absorbing material. Excessive fat is deposited in the body as adipose tissue, which is an emergency energy resource in starvation conditions. Continual excessive fat leads to obesity and its accompanying problems. Budgerigars obtain their fats in the form of vegetable oils found in many seeds. Some seeds contain more oil than others, so a balance must be struck between the types of seeds given.

Proteins:

These provide materials for growth, repair and replacement of body tissues. Like fats and carbohydrates, they are composed of molecular structures of carbon, hydrogen and oxygen. In addition, they

"Continual excessive fat leads to obesity and its accompanying problems."

have nitrogen, and sometimes sulfur or phosphorus. They are essential constituents of all living cells. The greatest part of the protein ratio for budgerigars is found in the seed.

Vitamin A:

Also known as retinol, vitamin A is necessary for growth in young birds. It is also vital for optimum function of the eyes and for protection of the mucus membranes. The major source of this vitamin is in green food.

Vitamin B Complex:

There are a number of vitamins in the B complex group. The most important are thiamine, riboflavin and nicotinic acid. Most of the B group vitamins are found in various bird seeds. A deficiency is virtually unknown in budgerigars fed a varied diet.

Vitamin C:

This is an important vitamin. It is found in fruit and green vegetables. It is also known as ascorbic acid. A deficiency can lead to various complications, including stunted growth,

bleeding of the mucus membranes and loss of resistance to infectious diseases.

This very beautiful variety of budgerigar is a normal cinnamon violet.

Vitamin D:

This vitamin plays an important part in the laying down of calcium and phosphorus in the bone structures. A deficiency in nestlings leads to rickets (malformation of the bones). Most vitamin D is manufactured in the body by the action of sunlight on the adult birds. It is transferred to the unborn young through the egg yolk. Vitamin D does not naturally occur in vegetable foods, so any additional supply must come from egg food or from vitamin supplements. An additional supply of this vitamin is particularly important to birds bred indoors.

Vitamin E:

Also known as tocopherol, this vitamin was first identified as being essential for the normal fertility of rats. It can be assumed to be necessary for the normal metabolism of budgerigars. Fortunately, it is found in bird seeds in relatively high quantities.

Vitamin K:

This is vital for the clotting mechanism of blood to function properly. Vitamin K is found in many green plants and vegetables.

Mineral Salts:

Like vitamins, mineral salts are a small but essential part of the diet. They are sometimes referred to as trace elements and form the inorganic part of the diet. A great number of minerals are required for the body to function properly for a variety of reasons:

1. As constituents of the bones (the rigid structures supporting the muscular system), beaks, nails, feathers and egg shell. The main minerals in this group include calcium, phosphorus and magnesium.
2. As constituents of the body cells of which muscle, blood corpuscles, liver and so on are composed. These include iron, sulfur, potassium and phosphorus.
3. As soluble salts which give the body fluids their composition and stability essential to life. These include sodium, potassium and chlorine.
4. As factors involved in chemical reactions in the body, especially those concerned with the release of energy during metabolism. These include phosphorus, magnesium and iron.

In addition to the foregoing minerals mentioned, a number of others are required in minute quantities. These are comprised of iodine, cobalt, copper, and molybdenum.

Foods and Feeding

Budgerigars are not difficult birds to feed; all of the basic nutrients are included in a mixture of seeds, green food, fruits, and a vitamin supplement. In the wild, the major part of a budgerigar's diet is the seeds of various grasses. The birds supplement this with the seeds and buds of all manner of weeds, shrubs and trees. It is likely that they consume insect and other invertebrate food as they forage among the food plants. This feeding strategy instinctively ensures that a wild budgie has a balanced diet.

It is all but impossible to provide a captive budgie with the type and variety of foodstuffs found in the wild. Therefore, a compromised diet must be offered. This diet still contains a variety of items to guarantee a good balance of nutrients.

Seed:

The staple part of the captive diet is seed, especially millet and canary seed. Special budgerigar mixtures are available in pet shops. These are comprised of a dealer's idea of a balanced diet for the birds. For large colonies of budgies, it may be less expensive to buy quantities of individual seeds and make

Spray Millet is enjoyed by all birds, and parakeets are no exception. This special treat is not only nutritious for the birds to eat but fun as well! Available at pet stores everywhere. Photo courtesy of Hagen Products.

up your own mixture. These can then be varied throughout the year depending upon whether your birds are breeding or molting.

Like people, budgerigars are individualistic in their feeding habits. While one bird may be crazy about millet, another may prefer sunflower seed. The following examples outline two suitable staple diets. The first is richer in protein and fat than the second. It is suitable for offering during the breeding season and the molt. During breeding, it ensures that the parent birds are well equipped for the strenuous tasks of courting, mating, egg producing, brooding, and rearing the young. It also warrants that the young receive adequate nutrients for growth. During molting, the diet aids in producing a strong renewal of plumage. Outside of the breeding and molting seasons, the birds require a lighter diet which will not promote obesity.

Diet 1 (to be given during breeding and molting)
55% various millets
35% canary seed
5% oats
2% niger

Diet 2 (to be given during the resting period)
60% various millets
32% canary seed
3% oats
3% hemp
2% niger

Note: Hemp should not be given in greater percentages than those stated. It has a very high oil (fat) content and excessive quantities lead to obesity and poor breeding results. Other seeds which may be given occasionally in small quantities are rape, maw, and linseed. The following table is an analysis of nutrients in various seeds.

Do not buy seed in larger quantities than your budgies will eat in a three to four week period. Old seed has less nutritional value than fresh seed and so is not as valuable to a bird's diet. Seed should be stored in

Allow your budgerigar ample time to eat and enjoy his meal before taking him out of his cage for a taming or training session.

airtight and waterproof containers and kept in a dry, well-ventilated area. With greater quantities of seed, an efficient means of storage must be employed. Many aviculturists include a special storage space for seed in their bird rooms or incorporate it in the shelter part of outside aviaries.

The seed may be fed to the birds in stainless steel, aluminum, porcelain or glass containers or hoppers. Plastic accessories are safe, but they tend to become pitted quickly and are easily broken. Also, there is the danger of a bird gnawing at the plastic and ingesting a

piece. Self-filling hoppers are useful in that a ration of seed for a few days' time can be supplied. Daily removal of seed husks from the feeding surface is mandatory. This is done by simply stirring the surface of the seed and gently blowing the husks away. Since budgies shell the seeds before swallowing the

Your pet shop carries a wide variety of budgie food items. When purchasing seed food, the fresher it is, the better it is for your pet: the nutritional value of a seed diminishes with age.

Nutrient Analysis of Seeds

	% Protein	% Oil/Fat	% Carbohydrate	% Mineral Salt
Canary Seed	13.8	4.9	52.1	2.2
Millet	11.2	3.9	61.5	3.0
Niger	17.5	32.7	15.4	6.9
Rape	19.5	41.0	10.3	3.9
Maw	17.0	40.3	12.2	5.9
Linseed	25.0	39.5	18.0	5.7
Oats	12.5	5.9	62.5	3.0
Sunflower Seed	16.0	22.0	21.0	2.5
Wheat	11.0	2.0	70.0	1.8

kernel, the empty husks tend to fall back into the food container. Eventually, the empty husks cover the uneaten seed entirely.

Open seed dishes must be emptied and cleaned at regular intervals. Do not locate them directly below a perch or the food is quickly soiled by droppings. The most suitable spot in the aviary is on a feeding platform, under the covered part, to prevent rain from wetting it.

Soaked Seed:

Soaking seed in water for 24 hours induces germination. Chemical changes within the seed occur, causing protein levels to increase and the seed contents to become more easily digestible. Soaked seed is an excellent dietary supplement for budgies, especially nestlings, as the nutritional value is increased. Soaked seed is also a good tonic for birds suffering from stress, particularly from a change in accommodation, and during treatment or recovery from a disease.

All sorts of bird seeds are suitable for soaking. You may desire to soak a mixture

A lovely array of budgerigars. A nutritious, well-balanced diet will be reflected in the quality and condition of your budgie's plumage.

which is already made up, or to prepare individual types to be given on a rotational basis. Only a very small amount of seed, enough for one day, should be prepared at a time. Soaked seed sours quickly and could thus cause stomach upset.

Place the required amount of seed in a container of cold water so that the grains are freely floating. Stir the mixture around to thoroughly wet each grain. Place the dish in a warm spot and allow it to sit. After 24 hours, drain and rinse the seed in clean, cold water. Serve it to your flock in a shallow dish. Any uneaten seed must be discarded at the day's end.

"Soaked seed is an excellent dietary supplement for budgies, especially nestlings, as the nutritional value is increased."

Sprouted Seed

Some of the soaked seed can be laid out on a damp paper towel. Keep the towel damp until the seed begins to sprout. This new growth is also a choice dietary supplement for any budgie.

Millet Sprays:

For the avicultural trade, these are the natural 'ears' from the living millet plant. Quantities of the sprays are dried out, without being thrashed. A more natural pattern of feeding is accomplished by supplying a certain amount of a bird's diet with sprays. Budgerigars delight in removing the seeds from the sprays, much in the same manner as they would forage for seeds in the wild. The sprays can be tied or clipped to the cage or aviary wire so that the birds derive exercise from clambering about to remove the seeds. Millet sprays may also be soaked and prepared in the same way as ordinary seed. These sprays should be given conservatively, though, as there is a danger that the variety of seed in the dishes will be ignored.

Green food and Fruit:

Budgerigars should be given a regular supply of various green food and fruit to round out their staple diet of seeds. Fresh green food and fruit contain a number of vitamins in greater quantity than that found in seeds. Spinach, carrots, apples, turnip, cabbage, peas, and many other fruits and vegetables are ideal. Not all birds will accept everything when first offered, though. So

experiment to find out what treats are your pet's favorites. Offer only one unusual item a day in a small amount. Too much and too sudden a change in a budgie's diet can cause intestinal upset. Simply wedge a piece of banana, pear or plum between the cage wires. Soon most budgies will be happily nibbling at their new treats.

Seeding grasses in season are eagerly accepted and highly nutritious. Weeds, such as chickweed, groundsel, shepherd's purse, dandelion and plantains, have value when given in small amounts. When collecting wild green food, be sure that no poisonous plants are hidden in the bundle. Avoid collecting near traveled areas where plants may be polluted by vehicle fumes and animal droppings. Never use anything which you suspect has been treated with insecticides, herbicides or artificial fertilizers. Bundles of green food can be secured with a clothespin or a piece of string. If suspended high up on the cage wire, a bird derives some exercise from pulling pieces off.

Tidbits:

Many budgie fanciers delight in giving their pets tidbits. Act with restraint, though, as a bird could get into the habit of eating only food which is detrimental in large quantities. Cakes, wholemeal breads, and breakfast cereals make a great feast.

One treat budgies enjoy is made as follows: Dissolve one teaspoonful of honey in five teaspoonsful of warm milk, then mix with enough plain sponge cake to form a semi-runny paste. Given in a small dish, this is quite nutritious. It can be offered to sick birds as a tonic or can be given as a dietary supplement to breeding birds.

Grit and Cuttlefish Bone:

The digestive system of any bird demands that it has grit in its gizzard. The bird swallows small stones, pieces of gravel and other insoluble materials to use for grinding food into a fluid mass for further digestion. The grit itself remains in the gizzard. Birds also extract valuable trace elements from the grit as it is gradually worn down by the muscular action of the

gizzard walls. A bird with no grit is unable to properly digest its food and soon becomes anemic.

Grit consists of a mixture of crushed stones, seashells, and cuttlefish bone. Bird sand, supplied for use on cage floors, may also contain a proportion of grit. Grit is best served in a dish separate from the regular food. In this way, you can readily monitor the amount of grit taken in.

Calcium is one of the most important minerals in a budgie's diet. It is essential for forming strong eggshells and the bones of growing chicks; it is also important in feather growth. A convenient way of supplying additional calcium is to offer cuttlefish bone. This is the internal skeleton of the squid-like cuttlefish. It is rich in

It is a poor practice to let bird seed accumulate on the floor of your budgie's cage. The conscientious hobbyist will keep his pet's quarters as clean as possible.

cuttlefish bone helps to keep beaks trim.

Cuttlefish bone is available in pet shops. Sometimes the skeleton can be found on the seashore, but this needs to be treated to remove dirt and sea-salt before being clipped into the cage. Soak the cuttlefish bone in running water for 48 hours, then dry it out thoroughly in the sun.

Other Supplements and Tonics:

An assortment of proprietary brands of vitamin and mineral supplements can be bought from avicultural suppliers. These vary in quality and effect, so it is best to select only well-known brands with a proven track record. Vitamin/mineral tonics are particularly useful during breeding and molting seasons. Supplements come in several forms: as fluids for adding to drinking water; as powders for adding to the food; and in blocks for clipping to the cage wire. Use supplements according to the manufacturer's instructions; an overdose of certain vitamins or minerals is more dangerous than supplying none at all.

A playful, inquisitive budgie.

calcium salts as well as a small quantity of other trace elements. Chewing at

Water:

Water is a part of the diet critical to life. Indeed, water forms at least 90% of all living organisms. Hence, fresh drinking water must be available to a budgie at all times. It can be given in a special pot or water fountain. The container must be cleaned and replenished daily.

A nice effect for an outdoor aviary is a 'pond.' One can be constructed from concrete. Prepare a small quantity of concrete (say 1 shovelful of cement to 2 shovelfuls of sand and 3 of crushed stone) and mix to a workable consistency with water. Place the concrete on top of a waterproof polyethylene sheet in a slight hollow in the aviary floor. Shape, by using a trowel, to form a shallow depression. For added strength, some galvanized mesh can be placed inside the concrete. Smooth the cement over with a soft brush before it sets. This makes the pond easier to clean later. For a more natural look, include a few rocks around the border.

If birds are already in residence when the pond is built, protect it with a piece of wire mesh while it sets. If the pond is constructed in very hot weather, cover it with damp sacking while it is setting. This prevents the concrete from drying out too quickly and cracking.

Once set, fill the pond with water and let it stand for 24 hours. Now scrub the surface thoroughly to remove lime deposits. Only now is the pond ready for use. It should be swept out daily with a fiber broom and the water freshened. At regular intervals, the water should be drained and the concrete surface scrubbed with a mild solution of bleach.

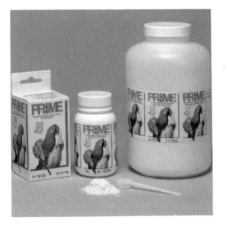

Breeding Budgerigars

To many enthusiasts, the most satisfying aspect of keeping budgies is breeding them. Many experienced breeders started off with a single pet bird. They became so fascinated with it that they decided to branch into breeding as a hobby. However, a pet bird is not always an ideal breeder and is content to remain a pet. If you want to breed budgerigars, obtain fresh stock specially for that purpose.

Nothing is more exciting than when your first breeding pair of budgies goes to nest—to see the first eggs and to hear the chirping of the young when they hatch. Fortunately, budgies are one of the easiest of all cage birds to breed. As long as you have a true pair and they have access to a nest box, it would be difficult to hold them back. Occasionally, there arises an incompatible pair or one that is infertile. This is quite disappointing if it should happen in your early

breeding attempts, but try again with a different pair or a different partner.

Sex Determination

The first requirement in breeding budgies is, of course, that you have a true pair. The adult cock's cere is bright blue (with the exception of red-eyed and recessive pied varieties which have purplish, flesh colored ceres) and that of the hen is brown. When in breeding

When planning which birds to mate, be sure to take genetic traits and behavioral idiosyncrasies into consideration. Naturally, any birds that you select for breeding should be in the best of health.

condition, the cock's cere becomes brighter blue, smooth and shiny. That of the hen becomes dark brown and rough. The sexing of youngsters is more difficult as the ceres are a pinkish-violet shade. Full adult plumage is achieved after the first molt at about four months of age. However, the ceres should have taken on their individual sex colors before this time.

Foundation Stock

Unlike most parrot-like birds, budgerigars are highly gregarious. They will breed

readily on the colony system providing a sufficient number of nest boxes is available. In the wild, it is not unusual to find many pairs of budgies breeding in several cavities in the same tree. Therefore, it is not unreasonable to expect them to nest in boxes set in close proximity when in captivity. Colony breeding in an aviary is a useful method for the beginner to learn more about the habits of the birds. The budgies will select their own mates, form a hierarchical system and generally behave in a natural manner. Budgies may squabble over mates and nesting sites, but they rarely injure each other in these encounters.

The youngsters bred from a colony will usually be good average specimens of mixed colors. It is unlikely that exhibition specimens will be produced. Prize stock is obtained through selective breeding, with a single pair of selected birds in a cage. It is better for a beginner to breed budgies first on the colony system in order to gain experience. Experiment with cheaper stock before breeding expensive stock from an exhibition line.

"Colony breeding in an aviary is a useful method for the beginner to learn more about the habits of birds."

When to Breed

Budgerigars will breed at almost any time of the year. However, do not allow them to breed in an outside aviary during colder parts of the year when there are likely to be more problems. Indoors, they can be bred summer or winter. Any pair, though, should not be permitted to rear more than three broods per annum as the parents will exhaust themselves. Most breeders stick to particular seasons in which to breed their stock. In the northern hemisphere, late February and the beginning of March seem ideal. Daylight is lengthening and green food is readily available. If breeding on the colony system, nest boxes can be given at this time. For selective breeding, the pairs can now be made up. Choose only those birds in the best condition.

Although cocks and hens reach sexual maturity as early as three or four months of age, do not breed any bird until it is at least 10 months old. Younger birds often make a hash of their breeding attempts, egg binding is more common and the offspring may be neglected.

Nestboxes

Whether birds are bred in cages or aviaries, good quality nestboxes are essential. In the wild, budgies breed in suitably sized hollows in vertical or horizontal tree branches, so the shape of the nestbox is really immaterial. Indeed, some breeders like to use hollowed out natural logs for their birds. In general, though, the majority prefer ordinary wooden boxes of uniform pattern for convenience.

The minimum internal measurements for a nest box are 15 x 15 x 23 cm (6 x 6 x 10 in). The entrance hole, about 4 cm (1.5 in) in diameter, is placed about 18 cm (7 in) from the bottom of a vertical box, or to the left or right end of a horizontal box. A short perch is set just below the entrance hole to give the birds easy access.

The nestbox may be fashioned from plywood or solid planking. Typically, the roof is hinged so that it can be opened for inspection of the contents. For cage breeding, it is more convenient to place the nestbox outside of the cage

50

to which the birds can gain access through a hole in the cage wall. For colony breeding, nestboxes should be set as high up as possible in the aviary flight. Each nestbox must be securely fastened so that there is no danger of its falling. They should all set at the same height to minimize fighting for the choicest location. If possible, provide more nestboxes than there are budgie pairs, to afford a wide selection.

As budgies do not build nests as such, a nest hollow should be provided. This is a separate piece of wood, fitting exactly into the base of the nestbox, into which a concave hollow is made. The diameter of the hollow is about 13 cm (5 in) and is placed in the center of the wood for a vertical box, or in one end of a horizontal box. The purpose of the concave is to keep the eggs in a convenient group for incubation.

Breeding Behavior

In temperate climates, lengthening of the daylight hours brings the birds into breeding condition (this can also be accomplished by artificial electric lighting). If breeding outdoors, it is best to wait until all chances of frost are over before introducing the nestboxes. When a nestbox is introduced, the hen shows the initial interest by sitting on the perch and peering inside. As the cock gets into the breeding mood, he becomes more excitable, running up and down the perches, constantly warbling, approaching the hen and preening her. He then starts to feed the hen with regurgitated food. If the hen is ready to breed, she accepts his advances. After a time, the hen enters the nestbox, often followed by the cock. At first, they continually enter and leave the box as if giving it a thorough inspection. Mating is soon accomplished, usually on a solid perch; the male hops onto the back of the female and positions his vent next to hers.

The clutch size varies from four to six eggs. At times there are as few as two or as many as ten. Five eggs seems to be the optimum number for a pair to brood and to rear. In the case of larger clutches, it is wise to foster

"As budgies do not build nests as such, a nest hollow should be provided."

time in the nestbox with her.

Incubation averages 18 days. Since the eggs are laid on alternate days, the young hatch in the same order. This means that with an average clutch of five, there is some ten days' difference between the hatching of the first and last chick.

When the chicks hatch, both parents feed them with regurgitated seed. Whatever the chick's age, the budgie pair gives each chick a fair quota of food. At this time, it is essential that the birds have a varied diet, including soaked seed and green food. When feeding the young, the hen apparently produces a proventricular secretion, sometimes called crop milk. An analysis of this fluid reveals that it is rich in protein.

The chicks develop rapidly. Naked at birth, they soon develop white down, followed closely by the first quills. They are ready to leave the nest in five to six weeks. The parents continue to feed them for a while after they fledge, but soon they are taking food independently. The chicks should now be moved to a separate accommodation.

With the variety of colors found in budgerigar genetics, the hobbyist can always look forward to the results that each particular mating will bring.

some of them to a pair with a smaller clutch. The eggs are white and about 2.0 x 1.6 cm (0.79 x 0.63 in). They average 2.2 grams in weight. One egg is laid every other day. The cock does not usually share in the incubation, but he does feed the hen and spends a lot of

Banding

Serious budgie breeders ring their young birds with closed metal rings. Each chick then has a permanent, individual number. This is important when breeding exhibition birds so that pedigrees are recorded and a permanent record is kept in a stock register. Local avicultural societies can advise you as to where to obtain rings. The rings are usually made from aluminum with initials and serial numbers embossed onto them. Rings are also available in colors.

The rings are fitted onto the leg of a chick when it is about one week old. If you do it earlier than this, the ring will probably just fall off; if you do it later, you probably will not be able to get the ring on! To attach the ring, hold the chick in one hand. Apply a little petroleum jelly to the toes of the leg to be ringed. Pass the ring over the front two toes, then over the leg and the back two toes. Wipe away

the petroleum jelly with a soft cloth.

As the chicks are ringed, the numbers should be recorded immediately in the stock register under the correct parentage. In this way, a useful record of pedigrees and other important notes is built up.

Breeding Problems

The breeding season should be relatively problem-free. The main problems which arise occasionally include infertile eggs, dead-in-the-shell and egg binding. This latter condition is

In becoming acquainted with a budgie, keep all movements slow and careful, so as not to frighten the bird.

potentially fatal. An egg-bound hen cannot pass the egg easily through the oviduct, takes on a disconcerting appearance and sits with her feathers fluffed out. She must be treated without delay.

The afflicted hen should be placed in a warm environment, such as a hospital cage, maintained at a temperature of about 30 C. In many cases, this heat treatment alone is enough to help successfully pass the egg. In stubborn cases, a veterinarian should be consulted as soon as possible. Birds suffering from egg binding should not be bred again for at least one year.

There are several possible causes of this condition, most of which are preventable. They include shortage of calcium, chilling and immaturity of the hen. In the case of a calcium deficiency, the eggs may have a soft, rubbery shell.

Failure of the eggs to hatch is a fairly common occurrence. This can be caused by the pair being infertile, immature, or being of the like sex. Various technical reasons may also

"Birds suffering from egg binding should not be bred again for at least one year."

The budgerigar has been a favorite pet bird for over a century, since its discovery in Australia.

apply. In some cases, one or more eggs in a clutch are infertile, while others hatch normally.

You can test for fertile eggs after they have been brooded for four or five days. Simply cut a small hole, just large enough to take an egg, in a piece of thick cardboard. Hold the egg in the hole in front of a strong light. A fertile egg shows a dark embryonic shadow. It is pink in color and blood vessels may be visible. An infertile egg has no shadows and appears yellowish. This technique is referred to as candling.

Chicks sometimes die in the shell. This can be caused by a variety of factors, including dietary deficiency in the hen, irregular brooding (the eggs may have chilled if the hen left the nest for too long) or poor humidity in the nest box. Poor humidity causes the eggs to lose moisture and the embryos desiccate and die. Breeding birds should have access to a bath so that they can wet their feathers and carry moisture back to the nest. Poor humidity problems are unlikely with outdoor breeding. Birds bred indoors should be kept under close observation. Birds refusing to bathe should be sprayed regularly with a fine mist of warm water.

Hygiene and Health

Most people know what is meant by good or bad health. Certainly, if you keep budgerigars, you want to keep them in the best of health at all times. You can go a long way in achieving this goal by practicing good standards of avicultural hygiene.

Hygiene is the science, or art, of preserving good health, or preventing disease and bad health. It is of the utmost importance when keeping groups of birds in close confinement. Infectious diseases can spread rapidly from one bird to the next. Therefore, strict and logical hygienic measures must be taken. This often sounds more complicated than it actually is. All that is really required is to keep birds in good health through thoughtful and thorough husbandry. Provided with the correct nourishment and kept in clean, dry, draft-proof and vermin-free quarters, budgies should

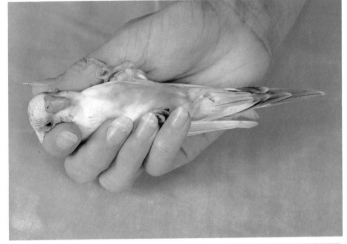

remain in good health for their entire lives.

Choosing Stock

A basic rule in avicultural hygiene is that you must ensure that the original and subsequent stock acquisitions are in good health at the outset. Stock should be obtained only from approved dealers and breeders; untidy or dubious premises must be avoided. Select your own birds personally. Never have them delivered or ordered by phone. Select birds that are clean, alert, bright-eyed and

It is advisable to check your budgie regularly for mites and other external parasites.

full colored. The plumage should be tight and neat. Avoid birds with ruffled feathers or bald patches. Choose a bird that takes an interest in its surroundings. Pass up one that sits and mopes in a corner.

Handle the budgie to make a close examination before

Note the smooth, even quality of this budgie wing. Your pet's plumage can sometimes be an indicator of illness or disease.

you purchase it. Handle it gently but firmly, gripping the whole body around the wings. Restrain the head between your fingers. The vent should be clean, with no signs of wetness or crusty material. Unfurl the wings to check for deformities or injuries. Look at the eyes, nostrils and mouth for signs of unusual discharge. Blow

softly into the feathers to look for external parasites or skin blemishes. Having ascertained that the prospective purchase is apparently healthy, it can now be taken home.

Budgies are usually placed in a box for the trip home. Do not be tempted to sneak a peek at the bird during the transport. Your new pet could easily be lost in this way. Do not keep the bird in the box any longer than absolutely necessary, though. Your budgie's new living quarters should already be set up before you bring the bird home.

Quarantine

New acquisitions should undergo a period of quarantine before introducing them to any existing stock. Quarantine is an isolation period which allows you time to spot developing diseases only in the incubation stage at the time of purchase. Quarantine accommodations must be kept well away from established stock for a minimum of two weeks. Should any disease develop, keep the bird isolated until it is completely cured.

58

Diseases and Treatment

Budgerigars are susceptible to an assortment of diseases. Fortunately, an outbreak is an exception rather than the rule in a well-kept establishment. Should a bird fall ill, though, it is wise to know what steps to take.

An ailing bird often sits moping in a corner or at the end of a perch. Its plumage is fluffed out and its head may be tucked under its wing. The budgie has a loss of appetite, then weight. Its condition can rapidly deteriorate. Such symptoms occur with many diseases. Should you be unsure about the disease in question or its treatment, immediately consult a veterinarian.

Place an obviously sick bird in an isolation cage away from other stock. A warm, dry, draft-proof area, preferably in semi-darkness, is ideal. Many ailing birds quickly respond to quiet, rest and heat treatment. Therefore, it is an asset to have a hospital cage as part of your standard equipment. Such a cage should be covered with glass or plexiglas to prevent drafts and to retain heat. The heat source can be a light bulb or heating pad. The temperature should be maintained around 32 C. The favorite food of your budgie should be placed in a container within easy reach of the bird. Fresh water must always be available.

An ailing budgie is customarily reluctant to feed. All too often, it is the effect of starvation which is fatal, not the disease itself. The budgie should therefore be enticed to eat by offering it the choicest tidbits. In the case of a stubborn bird, it must be handfed. A suitable mixture for producing energy and fighting disease is made by mixing a teaspoon of honey into a cup of hot milk. Add a beaten egg yolk and a pinch of salt. Mix this thoroughly and allow it to cool to a lukewarm temperature. It can be

Preening is one of the budgerigar's favorite activities. A budgerigar will preen a companion with the same gusto with which he preens himself.

administered by picking the budgie up in the hand and gently encouraging it to eat. An eye dropper permits small drops to be placed in the bird's mouth. Alternatively, the fluid can be dribbled into the bird's mouth from a teaspoon.

Mechanical Injuries:

Fractures or wounds are relatively uncommon. If they do occur, isolate the injured budgie and consult a veterinarian. A fractured bone in the leg can be repaired with a small splint and adhesive plaster. Wings may be set in position with adhesive tape alone. Splints are left in position for seven to eight weeks to allow the fracture to heal. Minor flesh wounds can be bathed with a mild solution of antiseptic. A veterinarian should be called in cases of heavy bleeding or extensive lacerations.

Overgrown Claws and Beaks:

Birds having access to perches of varied diameters and plenty of chew toys are unlikely to be afflicted with either of these problems. Occasionally they do occur and should be treated before developing into a fatal situation. Overgrown nails can simply be trimmed using sharp nail scissors or clippers. The toes should be held up to a light so that the quick, or blood vessel, to the nail can be seen. Take great care to ensure that the quick is not severed as profuse bleeding occurs. If this should happen accidentally, stop the bleeding by applying a styptic pencil or alum to the cut.

An overgrown beak can be a major problem as eventually the bird is unable to feed properly. A budgie will starve if the beak is left untreated. The beak can be trimmed to a near normal shape using nail clippers. This is a more difficult procedure than correcting overgrown claws. It is advisable to consult a veterinarian.

Head study of a lutino budgerigar. Many hobbyists consider this striking yellow bird one of the prettiest of all the budgie varieties.

Exhibition

Many people who have kept and bred budgies for some time like to enter the results of their efforts in competition. Showing budgerigars which you have bred is an exciting and challenging dimension to the bird-keeping hobby.

The first step in exhibiting budgies is joining a club or society. Most large towns have at least an avicultural society with a section devoted to budgerigars. Some towns even have budgerigar societies in their own right. Additionally, many countries have national societies or federations of societies. These organizations establish the rules, regulations and standards with respect to exhibiting birds.

Do not underestimate the importance of selecting, preparing and training birds for exhibition. A bird stands little chance of winning a prize if it is simply lifted from an aviary, put into a show cage and displayed. Well before the actual show season begins, the most promising looking birds must be selected. They are placed into stock cages to get them used to a more confined space.

Initially, breeding cages are suitable for this purpose. Four to six birds can be placed into each cage for training. (The sexes must be housed separately.) After a week, the birds can be introduced to the exhibition cages. These can be hung over the door of the stock cage. A millet spray or green food can be set in the exhibition cages to entice the birds to enter. As soon as the birds freely enter and leave the exhibition cage, they can be shut in for a short period of time. The time is steadily increased until the birds are quite at home in the exhibition cage.

During exhibition cage training, the birds occasionally should be sprayed with lukewarm water. A fine mist shower gets their plumage into a fine, silky condition. After spraying, the birds should be returned to dry quarters. It is best to spray the birds early in the day so they have plenty of time for drying out before nightfall.

Eventually, each bird should spend time in the exhibition cage on its own. Give it plenty of attention so it gets used to people peering at it through the wire front. A bird comfortable when people are in close proximity to it has a better chance of winning than a bird continually panicking or hiding in a corner.

Show cages come in varying standards, depending on the society or country. Most exhibition authorities are firm when it comes to the correct type of cage. A typical exhibition cage for budgies is of the box type. It has a wire front, is much smaller than a normal stock cage and is designed for a single bird. There are two short perches and the door is at one of the ends. The food and water pots are fitted into a special hatch in a panel below the wire front. Such cages are normally painted glossy black on the outside and white on the inside. The cage wire is white enamel.

Special carrying boxes are available to transport a number of cages. During travel, ensure that the birds are comfortable. They should not be subjected to stressful drafts or frights. Otherwise, your chances of winning may be ruined even before the birds arrive at the exhibition. A bird with the slightest blemish is just as well withdrawn. Many exhibition authorities inspect birds before allowing them entrance to the exhibition hall. The officials want to prevent the spread of infectious diseases throughout the rest of the contestants.

Index